Inside
Job

T0345789

Books by John Skoyles

Poetry
A Little Faith
Permanent Change
Definition of the Soul
The Situation

Prose
Generous Strangers
Secret Frequencies: A New York Education
A Moveable Famine: A Life in Poetry

Inside
Job

John Skoyles

Carnegie Mellon University Press
Pittsburgh 2016

Acknowledgments

Grateful acknowledgment is made to the following journals and anthologies where many of these poems first appeared:

B O D Y: "Music Appreciation"
Freshwater Review: "The Weaker the Wine"
Hotel Amerika: "After Tanikawa," "He's Had It," "The Beech Forest"
Ibbetson Street: "Nunc," "Quarry," "Rhubarb, Rhubarb"
Jung Journal: Culture and Psyche: "Academe," "Despair," "Granville," "Inside Job,"
    "No Surprises," "Portrait of a Portrait Painter"
The American Poetry Review: "Bachelor of Arts," "Borges," "Capitalism,"
    "Dinnertime in Elmhurst, Queens," "The Friday Night Fights,"
    "Grace Paley," "Hypnotized," "In Memory of a Marriage," "My Fascist
    Grandmother," "Philosophy 101," "Say When: Stanzas on Cancer," "St.
    Bartholomew's School," "Turkish Taffy"
The New Yorker: "Autobiography"
Plume: "Coal Bin," "Killer," "The List," "The Human Canary," "Spite Fence"
Salt Hill Journal 28: "Friday Night with My Dead Friends"

Devouring the Green: Fear of a Human Planet: An Anthology of New Writing (Jaded
    Ibis Press, 2015): "Evolutionary Shenanigans"
Good Neighbors: The Democracy of Everyday Life in America (Princeton University
    Press, 2016): "Spite Fence"
Liberation: New Works on Freedom from Internationally Renowned Poets (Beacon
    Press, 2015): "First Drink"
The Plume Anthology of Poetry 3 (MadHat, Inc., 2015): "Christmas Special: Stanzas
    on Alzheimer's"

Cover art: Pat de Groot, *sunny day*, 2000, oil paint on panel, 12 x 11 inches,
courtesy the artist and Albert Merola Gallery

Book design: Connie Amoroso

Library of Congress Control Number 2016930371
ISBN 978-0-88748-614-2

for Michael Ryan

Contents

I.

II.

III.

a man keeps pouring grape into ORANGE
and orange into the one marked GRAPE,
pouring orange into GRAPE and grape into ORANGE forever.

—Muriel Rukeyser

I.

Autobiography

I did not lead my life
although my life followed me,

not in lockstep or formed flight
but in the second line,

calling me new names,
Mr. Danke Schoen,

Dr. I'm Sure It's Nothing.
A parade of sorts

because isn't life
just one person after another,

a whispering campaign
of family sayings:

"At the top of the mountain,
keep climbing,"

and "Thunder's the promise,
fulfillment's the rain."

Behind me, redheaded girls from Chelsea
whose collars match their cuffs,

a trip to Itchycoo Park,
and the cats Mirabelle and Edward

who wake me at dawn
though both are dead.

Yes, it rained
but there were not a lot

of tears, only a very large one
breaking over everything.

Dogs barked but the parade
went on, and a life followed me

though I did not lead my life.

My Fascist Grandmother

after Curzio Malaparte

My fascist grandmother
would have loved
your books—

she used to sing
Mussolini's "Giovinezza"
to the shanty,

the lace curtain,
and the two-toilet
Irish in Queens.

Teodolinda Pioselli Bertolotti,
my fascist grandmother
whom I loved

and not just for
the heaving rigatoni
quality of her name

but because her bosom,
which preceded her
into every room,

shaped a soft sofa
for my migraines
that came

from watching her
march a knife
into the backyard

chickens,
bleeding a slit neck
through a funnel.

My fascist grandmother
would have loved
your books of vengeance

because on Judge Street
vengeance was hers,
pouring bleach along

the stoop to drown
the bitter red colonies.
When I grew long hair

and wore
a McCarthy button,
she dismissed

my hippie look
at the kitchen door
with the shake of a spoon.

My fascist grandmother
would have loved
your books.

Dinnertime in Elmhurst, Queens

Mothers lean on the slate sills
of our railroad flats
and shout for Charlie, Wally,
Howard, Paul.

Mine whistles since she's lost her voice.

The Irish crunch saltines
into tomato soup.
The Poles scoop the huge oily cabbage.

My parents' bedspread
holds the floury remains
of dried ravioli
now boiling in a bath of steam.

All of this so long ago . . . we hated to go home.

My children call me to the kitchen.
It's true. I'm late.

The glass of whiskey on the end table
has blocked the face of the clock.

Coal Bin

Some witchy and slinky,
ready to coo on a pillow,

others nun-like, eyes open
with the wonder of a startled

sleepwalker—all bluntly bare.
My uncle stashed his harem

of goddess statues
in our coal bin

where I caught him
at the casement

turning his bronze minxes
and virgins this way

and that, as innocent
as the slow boy next door

who spun a huge top
by a string above his lap

as he sang the hymn
about shepherds and sheep

on that street that was less
pasture and more tray

of ashes stubbed out
by the hand of the lord.

First Drink

No one destroyed the day.
It died in its own good time.

Someone killed the dusk,
my parents' tilt-a-whirl

through the kitchen's
thrown-down plates

and carving knives.
Uncle Fred gave life

to night, taking me in,
pouring more than a little

gin into my Squirt,
a citrus drink

like its rival
Wink,

that sent me
to the beach's

sweaty threshold
between salt and sweet.

A second glass,
and all the parts

of speech shoved off to sea,
leaving me alone

with the infinitive
to drink.

Bachelor of Arts

Burglars and spiders along
the fire escape, the shaggy
horsehair sofa, the hatchet
my father insisted taking
with him to his coffin—
are these enough to say
what childhood meant to me
as I jerked and cursed my way
to a college named after
Galileo's prosecutor for whom
the world was a paradise
created by God and re-gifted
by the church who told us to thank
the One who marred the brains
of every black-robed beast
roaming the campus at night.
I changed into a hippie banshee
after answering the squeaky-sweet
call of the priest known
in Loyola dorm as X,
ancient Father Francis Xavier,
and helped him to undress.

He's Had It

Something about his task to shoo
the hamster from its hiding place

behind the breadbox,
to hand the landlord

a bad check
while his parents threw dice

at Foxwoods. Something about
Mrs. Fortini hanging her wash

on their line, her spindly
underwear unruly

in the wind.
Something about the screens,

something about the flies,
something about some

trying to get out,
some trying to get in.

Best-Selling Poet Theatens My Love Life

My new girl's not the literary sort,
the owner of Pam's Pets,

with its feathers, fur and fin,
yet she calls to say

she's heard great poems on NPR
that made her laugh so hard

I can chart her swoon
at the poet's charm.

In the background, an African Grey
whistles the theme from

The Good, The Bad and the Ugly.
To me, the poet's best

are few and far between
but it's hopeless to quote

the *Times* review:
with him it's never a line

that counts, but always the anecdote,
the one about.

Pam asks, "Funny, don't you think?"
Should I say: Like the fire-eater

in the circus, to the public he's a freak,
but to the freaks he's not a freak?

No. Pam pours kibble into stainless steel,
she has no ideas but in things

and asks again, "Really funny, right?"
The Grey has switched to "Walk Away Renee"

and the well-heeled poet's
about to knock my love life

off its steady keel
but I've learned from tricksters

like Frost that there are ways
of telling the truth, and I resort

to one of them: a lie.
"Yes," I say. "Hilarious!

Are we on for tonight?"

Granville

My father might have won
the war with my mother
and named me Granville,
a crowned head
on a brass plate
along the law firm hall
he paced as a boy
delivering mail.
Runners-up were
Coverdale and Marsden,
heirs in plaid shorts
who waved from
Central Park's carousel,
then nudged their sailboats
further and further
from the sweltering shore.

Hypnotized

My grandmother called me to the porch
of our railroad flat which overlooked
backyard plots divided by discarded
window frames, Christmas trees, and
doors on their sides. She pointed
to a snake on the handrail, and a finch
on the post, saying the snake
had hypnotized the bird. Their eyes
were locked. I never paid attention
to those superstitious tales from her native Italy—
if a mouse frightened a pregnant woman
and she grabbed her throat in panic,
a rodent-shaped mark would appear
on the newborn's neck. I was thinking
about this when the bird flew toward
the snake who opened his mouth and swallowed it.

Killer

after Montale

When he saw me coming
from stickball
swinging a broom handle,
he'd call *Killer*
from his chair on the stoop.
Someone's grandfather,
a steam fitter who worked
weekends at Yankee Stadium
wiping box seats with a mitt.
Killer, he'd scrawl in the air,
calling attention to my skinny frame,
a stick carrying a stick.
When I go to hell,
I know he'll yell *Killer*
from his bench among the coals
and I'll wave
my kindling from the flames.

Nunc

The Latin word
I fell in love with
at choir practice
I printed on a card—

a naughty uncle,
bank account after
divorce, a bomb
surviving the plummet.

What do you have there?
Mrs. Rimmer, Choirmaster,
asked, confiscating
my world, confirming

my Catholic faith
in catastrophe
as she pointed
her beak at all of us

sopranos, reading aloud
the four letters—*Nunc!*
My past brought to the present.
Then suddenly now.

Someone, Somewhere

When I was a little girl,
little girl, little girl
When I was a little girl,
When, When, When
                    Childhood Street Song

No matter what science says,
or that priests and rabbis agree
everyone who lives must die,
my grandmother believes
someone, somewhere
will escape alive.
She trusts God to pull
a vengeful sleight of hand
on those who pass baskets
after sermons about
eternity. She's certain
there exists a little girl
jumping rope who never lands
on a crack, who curtsies
in a pretty dress after singing
When, when, when
while the rest of us fade
into age. Even a corpse
casts a shadow, Grandma
used to say, and she was not
a student of Swedenborg
or Blake, but a maker
of meatballs, a baker of cakes,
a lover of steak who swore
houseplants flinched
when she carved a roast
in their presence.

Just Go

Go to the graveyard
and look around,
you'll get the advice
you want from death's experts—
tomb festooners
who pinpoint their grief
by stabbing the earth
with wire stems, making
zigzagging bouquets
above the charcoal beds.
They come daily to place
pillows on headstones,
flags near the feet
of those who've gone
from warm to lukewarm,
to no heat at all on this planet
of careening ash, just dust.

Despair

Despair, sin greatest in the eyes
of the church, I'll always remember you

because I guessed murder number one
on some nun's 5th grade test

and you trailed me home
like the wires above the street

from which the stoplights swung,
cables I never noticed until that day

I saw you everywhere, even
in our vestibule's bright milk box

and lawn chairs stacked all winter,
the dead bolt lock, my key on a cord

that opened the door
I rushed through,

hoping my mother'd be home
so I could quiz her

on the greatest sin and there
she was, frosting a cake

for my father's birthday,
saying she hoped he liked it

because she'd forgotten the candles,
so I ran to Kresge's,

hoping to return in time
to have them lit when he walked in,

and I realized I was
full of hope, and so was she.

II.

Borges

The bookdealer collected Borges firsts,
so when that blind writer
lectured nearby, he stood on line
to have them signed.
Stacking each volume on the rostrum
and naming it,
the dealer clicked his pen,
handing it to Borges who said
even he did not own such rare works,
and clicked the pen again.
Too polite to comment, the dealer
walked away, every signature invisible.

Grace Paley

At Sarah Lawrence, a student gripes
that each morning when she tries
to write, nothing happens.
She sits and sits, and files her nails.
Sips more coffee, types a bit,
gets up to spray her failing plants.
"Grace," she asks in front of the class,
"Can you help?" Grace, her gray hair
in a bun, wearing a floral dress
and cracking gum, puts her hands
on her knees, leans toward the woman
and says, "Maybe you're just not a writer."
She looks around the room.
"Maybe she's just not a writer,"
she repeats. "Nothing wrong with that."

Philosophy 101

Blind Professor Hatch set the class
on edge each time he smoked.
Waving a lit match just under
his eye, he expertly applied
the flame to the tip.
After a strenuous test,
ten frat boys turned their backs
and dropped trou, mooning
the philosopher as he explained
Plato's cave, that the net of shadows
seen by the chained prisoners
is the closest to reality they'd ever get.

The Human Canary

Times Square

Before he became famous, Tiny Tim
sang falsetto in the basement
of Hubert's Freak Show
as Larry Love, the Human Canary.
He stood between Frito,
a midget scarred in a childhood fire,
and the hirsute, one-legged
Monkey Girl with two sets of teeth.
When he crooned, "Tears on My Pillow,"
You don't remember me, but I remember you . . .
a woman in the front row made
tsking sounds and said,
"Such sad things there are in this world."

Quarry

Heavyweight Irish Jerry Quarry
had a name that fit his years
of taking heavy hooks to the head:
an open pit mine
from which granite's dug,
a heap of game killed in a hunt.
Sick with Dementia Pugilistica
but somewhat rich at thirty-eight,
he turned to writing poetry.
Years later, entering the hall of fame,
and surrounded by men seeking
his autograph, he was in such pain
he couldn't lift a pen.

Spite Fence

My neighbor forced his abutter
to raze the warped and rotten fence
because he didn't want to see
the sagging wood when he sat
on the porch in the morning
having coffee with his wife.
The fence was removed, replaced
with something new, so now
the neighbor has breakfast
facing a row of garden gnomes,
some naked, and a few
of those anatomically correct.

Rhubarb, Rhubarb

Bunny Lang loathed the brash author
of a drama she directed,
so when he attended, she switched
the opening score to "The Elephant Polka."
And in the crowd scene, to mimic
the arousal of an angry mob,
she used the ancient stage trick
of asking half the cast
to mutter *rhubarb, rhubarb,*
and the rest *vichyssoise, vichyssoise.*
But this time, the audience fell
into endless glee, as she ordered
each word pronounced distinctly.

Capitalism

The publicity stunts of James Moran
included squatting on an ostrich shell
for twelve days to promote
The Egg and I, leading a bull
through a fine china shop off Fifth,
and changing horses midstream
to mock a flip-flopping mayor.
He tried to tout a candy bar by sending
midgets attached to kites across Midtown.
His permit denied, he said, "It's a sad day
when a man can't fly a midget over Central Park."

Turkish Taffy

My father rode an elevator
with Victor Bonomo,
inventor of Turkish Taffy
and author of its slogan
Smack It and Crack It.
Bonomo said it wasn't easy,
that before taffy he had
three failed candy bars:
"Thanks," "Hats Off," and "Call Again."
To keep the market going,
he began a campaign starring
puppets named Bo, No and Mo.
He confided to my father
that the taffy wasn't Turkish
and wasn't even taffy.

The Friday Night Fights

I watched the Friday night fights with my father
when I was a boy. We sat in overstuffed chairs
before an RCA console. As soon as
the bell rang, my father shuffled his feet,
bobbing, weaving, throwing uppercuts
and hooks as if he were in the ring.
I was afraid to look over, it seemed
pure madness. Sometimes my mother
arrived with bowls of ice cream, and called
him crazy. Today they call it the mirror neuron.

Music Appreciation

Conductor Andrew Heath never read
our term papers. We typed a first
and last page, filling the middle
with Our Fathers, Hail Marys,
the Gettysburg Address.
He lost his temper only once,
when a student who dominated
discussions clapped as a visiting cellist
finished a Brahms sonata.
That sweet sound, about to fade, died
in the know-it-all's premature applause.
Heath made strangling motions
at the offender's throat, saying,
"The last note is not the end—
the last note is the silence that follows."

St. Bartholomew's School

I was a great speller until I had Brother Jones
in 8th grade. A Franciscan, he wore a brown
hooded robe cinched at the waist with three knots
for poverty, chastity and obedience, but his
were always untied. He mispronounced words
as he marched down the aisles, saying *Finan-shu-wool*
for *Financial. Per-hib-mited,*
a mixture of Prohibited and Permitted.
Frothcoming. A pederast and sadist, he took
most of us twelve-year-olds to a room where
we were laid over a chair with our head
between his legs as he hit us on the buttocks
with a board, but no one said a word.
St. Bartholomew's School. Elmhurst, Queens. 1963.

The Beech Forest

The woods had the scent of the sea
and not the sea
alone, but wind above

and shell and sand below.
A young man humming
the *Norfolk Rhapsody*

walked past me, over oak
and maple leaves,
the ransacked tents

of slugs and snakes.
I paused for a word,
but he kept on until

the path skewed
and I lost him uphill,
feeling we had met before

we both were born,
long before
I was a father,

and he, a son
near the curdling sea
that would bring him

and take him away from me.

Say When: Stanzas on Cancer

When shadows laced his lungs,
night didn't fall, darkness rose

and my son went out hiking
with the gods.

When my son became your son, doctor,
I pushed a ladder toward the moon.

When my son became different from
your son, my friend,

we walked together through a mile
of dune he might not see again.

When my son came home,
he tossed the ball hour after hour

to the one who knew, pawing
and whining, that he could be dying.

After Tanikawa

A candle can be stolen,
but its flame can't be stolen.

A Vermeer can be stolen,
but his milkmaid can't be stolen.

A slogan can be stolen,
and an election, it's true, can be stolen.

Champagne can be stolen,
but the night they invented champagne
can't be stolen.

Experience can't be stolen
but life continues to be stolen.

Friday Night with My Dead Friends

I start by mimicking Sheridan's stride
toward the wet bar, where I fill
a glass in his honor. Shinder
shoulders through the drapes

toward Levis, whose early start
has him swaying under the ceiling fan.
I pour a healthy shot
for Dugan, sashay in Larry's

sluggish steps, and then
I imitate the fan,
windmilling my arms like Sara
singing "We're in the Money"

in pig latin, not church latin,
not that latin of the god
who spoke so little to so many,
but the one who wrote

the music of the spheres
and, secondhand, the symphony
that tingles the bones
of the dead in the living room

of their understudy.

In Memory of a Marriage

One is two:
drinker and drunk.

The other's also two:
drunk and ex-drinker.

Both are each
and two are neither.

Drink up!
says the evening.

Sober up!
says the sun.

Both are two
and neither each.

No Surprises

Summer traffic. Winter scorn.
Lengthy legs along the shore

sculpted by the god
who knows just what

his children want.
The shark of new love,

the wound from an old friend.
Reading between the lines

of swimsuits. The wish to plunge
from the Bourne Bridge.

What's the task of its tall fence?
What's the purpose of the sea?

The List

Branches shiver as if a wand
transformed them
into wands themselves,
the way our friends
become poplars
planted in their memory—
Steven Clover, Lon Scott,
Franco Palumbo,
jeweler, banker, chef.
There's no rest from the list
that grows each morning
as we face the sun
with a cool look
like we can handle
the digging and burying,
that we don't see every limb
on every tree
as a wing cut from flight.

Evolutionary Shenanigans

The proper study
of monkey-kind is man,
and the true study
of man is shenanigans.

Ask a priest,
a judge, or a cyborg,
especially a cyborg,
because he will show you

yourself
just as a good mirror
or a good actor
reflects a beast

part flesh and blood,
part make-believe.
One millennium at a time,
I study the monkey

and the cyborg studies me.

Portrait of a Portrait Painter

I don't need
a photograph
to recall her

looking into the lens,
shoulders against
the gallery wall,

beside her painting
of a bewildered girl,
one of her many girls,

always girls,
daring to come alive
and join the world

that halted
her as a girl,
checked by an arm

around her waist,
then pressed like a leaf
into a heavy book

as a marker
not of place,
but of time

when other girls
her age
began to thrive,

but she
would have to wait
for these girls

to arrive, all
having one name,
hers, and one face,

her face.

Da Vinci, De Gourmont, and Me

You thought she left
but she just vanished
into the sheets,

a white brocade
on a sheaf of loose leaf.
The angel you loved

and the strangled angel
came together
the way night

meets an extinguished lamp.
Nature, she sighed,
favors the male,

and she covered herself
with a pale chemise.
I stood by the bed,

lifting a book
from the shelf
that said the glow-

worm's a real worm,
it crawls, falls
and stands

on its head
to attract a mate
but remains

a larva,
not much of an animal,
a poor excuse for a clown.

Academe

Is the mockingbird drunk,
repeating himself like the chickadee,
like the Acting Chair
of the Acting Department
of the college I'm fleeing,
that superannuated professor
on a daiquiri spree whose syllables
melt like slush along chilled
cocktail glasses at dusk?
Yes, this bird's blitzed, zonked,
leaping when the telephone rings,
and he answers mimicking
that ring, confronting every
living thing as if he knows
Randall Jarrell wrote a poem about him,
as if he will never forget
I owe him for chasing a squirrel
down Mockingbird Lane
in front of my Malibu
when I myself was drunk,
driving out of Dallas for good
at midnight, keeping awake
by playing the Highwaymen,
lost until he led the way to I-35.
That was the last time
I saw Texas, the big red state
fading in my rearview,
but not the last I heard from
the Acting Chair, whose farewell
postcard of bluebells in bloom
contained the bright
hypocritical advice: Be yourself.

Inside Job

Suicide is an inside job
though something in the air
can kill you too—

a lifetime
turning doorknobs
left and right,

saying good morning,
good night,
standing among moths

along the lawn
at dusk
as they fly up

the funnel
of the flashlight beam,
relief rags

to those
bone alone
who mimic

that ultimate isolato,
the bachelor best man,
who raises

an after-dinner toast
at a wedding
where you're on the lawn

at dusk, and see
her again
too late to ask

what wrongs
brought the years
of wound and salve,

crime and lab,
the hurt
and the nurse

whose hug
is a clamp,
a lamp that illuminates

that damp head
of hair
after a rain shower

you lean through,
tangled in wet
brunette strands,

a curtain,
a closet,
a room with no view,

a path
in the dark,
a light in your hand

leading to you.

Christmas Special: Stanzas on Alzheimer's

my mother (1919—2014)

We sat on the couch
drinking tea and watching
Bing Crosby vouch

that Christ is King
while children pushed trucks
around our feet in rings.

She lifted my son,
kissed his chin,
and over music from accordions

said, *John,*
is Santa Claus for real?
Stunned by the question,

my wife gave her the task
of stringing popcorn to a thread
to keep her from asking

anything else, afraid the kids
might start doubting
St. Nick's stout slide

down our chimney. I joked
that Santa put on a few pounds
this year, and then she spoke

about Christmastime
as it used to be,
when elves in lines

stocked shelves behind Saks' window
and jolly men on every block
rang bells while yelling, *Ho Ho Ho!*

She repeated it,
flushed and proud
as if outfitted

in red and fluffy white—
three syllables
without foresight or hindsight.

The Weaker the Wine

after Su Tung-p'o

The weaker the wine,
the easier to drink twice as much.
The thinner the robe,
the better to wear it double.
Ugliness and beauty are opposites,
but when you're drunk,
one's as good as the other.
Bitchy wives and nagging mistresses,
the older they get, the more they're alike.
To reach your goals,
remain anonymous—
avoid the White House, Gracie Mansion,
political furor and the gossip
of windbags. A marriage can seem
to go on forever, but at last
it comes to an end. Meanwhile
it's no greater feat to be
a rich corpse or a poor one,
a dead drunk or a sober stiff.
Diamonds and pearls circle
the throats of dead celebrities
to preserve their looks.
It doesn't work, but after a thousand years
they feed the robbers of their tombs.
As for literature, it's its own reward.
Fortunately, fools pay no attention to it.
The chance for graft makes them sing with joy.
Good men are their own worst enemies.
Getting drunk is a foolproof reward
for doing good deeds, like rescuing
a sick cat who vomits on your sheets.

Throughout the universe, good and evil,
joy and sorrow, the purely pedigreed
and the rough mutt are simply aspects
of the Void.

2010

The Diminishing House, Nicky Beer
A World Remembered, T. Alan Broughton
Say Sand, Daniel Coudriet
Knock Knock, Heather Hartley
In the Land We Imagined Ourselves, Jonathan Johnson
Selected Early Poems: 1958-1983, Greg Kuzma
The Other Life: Selected Poems, Herbert Scott
Admission, Jerry Williams

2011

Having a Little Talk with Capital P Poetry, Jim Daniels
Oz, Nancy Eimers
Working in Flour, Jeff Friedman
Scorpio Rising: Selected Poems, Richard Katrovas
The Politics, Benjamin Paloff
Copperhead, Rachel Richardson

2012

Now Make an Altar, Amy Beeder
Still Some Cake, James Cummins
Comet Scar, James Harms
Early Creatures, Native Gods, K. A. Hays
That Was Oasis, Michael McFee
Blue Rust, Joseph Millar
Spitshine, Anne Marie Rooney
Civil Twilight, Margot Schilpp

2013

Oregon, Henry Carlile
Selvage, Donna Johnson
At the Autopsy of Vaslav Nijinksy, Bridget Lowe
Silvertone, Dzvinia Orlowsky
Fibonacci Batman: New & Selected Poems (1991-2011),
        Maureen Seaton
When We Were Cherished, Eve Shelnutt

The Fortunate Era, Arthur Smith
Birds of the Air, David Yezzi

2014
Night Bus to the Afterlife, Peter Cooley
Alexandria, Jasmine Bailey
Dear Gravity, Gregory Djanikian
Pretenders, Jeff Friedman
How I Went Red, Maggie Glover
All That Might Be Done, Samuel Green
Man, Ricardo Pau-Llosa
The Wingless, Cecilia Llompart

2015
The Octopus Game, Nicky Beer
The Voices, Michael Dennis Browne
Domestic Garden, John Hoppenthaler
We Mammals in Hospitable Times, Jynne Dilling Martin
And His Orchestra, Benjamin Paloff
Know Thyself, Joyce Peseroff
cadabra, Dan Rosenberg
The Long Haul, Vern Rutsala
Bartram's Garden, Eleanor Stanford

2016
Something Sinister, Hayan Charara
The Spokes of Venus, Rebecca Morgan Frank
Adult Swim, Heather Hartley
Swastika into Lotus, Richard Katrovas
The Nomenclature of Small Things, Lynn Pedersen
Hundred-Year Wave, Rachel Richardson
Where Are We in This Story, Sarah Rosenblatt
Inside Job, John Skoyles
Suddenly It's Evening: Selected Poems, John Skoyles